VIKINGS

A Drama

by

Steve Metcalfe

D1232213

S A M U E L   F R E N C H ,   I N C .

25 WEST 45TH STREET   NEW YORK 10036

7623 SUNSET BOULEVARD   HOLLYWOOD 90046

LONDON   *TORONTO*

"VIKINGS"
received its World Premiere
at the Manhattan Theatre Club
October 21, 1980

IMPORTANT ADVERTISING NOTE

ALL producers of VIKINGS shall announce the name of Steve Metcalfe as the author of the play in all programs distributed in connection with performances of the play as hereinafter set forth, and in all instances in which the title of the play appears for the purposes of advertising, publicizing or otherwise exploiting the play and/or a production thereof, the name of Steve Metcalfe must also appear on a separate line in which no other name appears, immediately beneath the title, and must appear in size of type not less than Fifty Per Cent (50%) the size of the title type.

IN ADDITION, producers must give the following acknowledgement on the first page of credits in all programs distributed in connection with performances of the play:

"VIKINGS"
received its World Premiere
at the Manhattan Theatre Club
October 21, 1980

This play is dedicated to my grandmother,
ELSE LARSEN BRIGHAM

MANHATTAN THEATRE CLUB

Artistic Director
LYNNE MEADOW

Managing Director
BARRY GROVE

presents

VIKINGS

by

STEVE METCALFE

with

SHEILA ALLEN   **TOM ATKINS**

BOYD GAINES   **WILLIAM SWETLAND**

Directed by
LYNNE MEADOW

Associate Director
GEORGE MEAD

Set Design
TONY STRAIGES

Costume Design
LINDA FISHER

Lighting Design
F. MITCHELL DANA

Production Stage Manager
VIRGINIA HUNTER

October 21, 1980 - November 30, 1980

MTC productions are made possible in part with public funds from the National Endowment for the Arts and the New York State Council on the Arts.

CAST
(*in order of appearance*)

Peter Larsen .... TOM ATKINS
Yens Larsen .... WILLIAM SWETLAND
Gunnar Larsen .... BOYD GAINES
Betsy Simmons .... SHEILA ALLEN

The action of the play takes place in and around the home of the Larsen family.

Standby for Gunnar Larsen—Richard Patrick-Warner, for Yens Larsen—William Cain, for Betsy Simmons—Gloria Maddox.

VIKINGS

ACT I

SCENE 1

PETER. I'm not completely sold on this idea. Don't any of you think I am. I don't mind people in my back yard or kitchen or living room—if you dropped by on the spur of the moment I might offer you a beer and a sandwich—I just happen to feel that there are rooms in a house you don't put on display to the general public. They're personal, private rooms and sometimes they're not as neat and well ordered as the parts of the house you show around. That's how I feel at any rate. Not that it makes much difference. I've been overruled two to one. Pretty goddamned slim victory, that's all I have to say. I should have expected it. The two of them have always been as thick as thieves. We might as well get on with it. This is my father, my son and me. The three of us were together for awhile. . . .

YENS. Listen! I'm Yens Larsen, this is Peter, this is Gunnar. I'd like to say right at the beginning. . . .

GUNNAR. Don't let this old buzzard get started. We're hardly going to be able to shut him up as it is.

YENS. How ungrateful children are. Especially grand-children.

GUNNAR. Would you listen to him?

YENS. You!

GUNNAR. You!

(*They laugh at some secret, shared joke.*)

PETER. About a year ago Yens got very sick . . .

7

GUNNAR. Legionnaire's Disease! He was struck with an uncontrollable urge to wear a fez!

PETER. It was unexpected to say the least. He was a strong, vibrant man, the patriarch of our family . . .

YENS. I wanted John Wayne to play this part!

PETER. May we please get serious?

YENS. Pay him no mind. He's always serious. He doesn't get it from me!

GUNNAR. Me either. Or, I should say, I didn't get it from him.

YENS. It was his mother. She had looks that could freeze black cats in their tracks. (*Pointing to* PETER, *who is glaring at him.*) Case in point. Go on, go on.

PETER. We're builders, carpenters. Houses mostly. When we can get them. We'll do any kind of general contracting work—additions, remodeling. I'll put in a new driveway if the price is right. But our specialty is houses.

YENS. Homes. Homes!

PETER. Yeah, all right. Homes.

YENS. Peter!

(YENS *crosses and whispers in* PETER's *ear.*)

PETER. Yeah, yeah . . . We're—Jesus, Dad—Vikings. I mean, not really, but we're Danish, and Yens—I'm not exaggerating, he does this constantly—calls us that. Vikings.

YENS. Listen. My son and grandson were born with a sixth finger on each hand!

GUNNAR. Oh God, you had to tell them that.

YENS. You should be proud!

PETER. Yens feels that's a special sign.

YENS. It is! It's the mark of the Vikings!

PETER. All we have to show for it is the scars. The sixth finger was removed. For Guns, a week after he was born; for me, when I was married at twenty.

There's not much call for Vikings these days, contrary to popular opinion. So now you know.

YENS. The birthdays.

PETER. Jesus.

GUNNAR. Wait till you hear this.

YENS. Birthdays! The three of us were born on the same day! Oh, what gifts, what presents! To have a *son* born on your birthday!? And then! Unto you this day a *grandson* has been born!!

GUNNAR. He loves to embarass me.

YENS. With six fingers!!

PETER. I'm warning you, pay no attention to him. He thinks he's perfect. It can drive you crazy. Sometimes the two of them send me running from the house, screaming. I have to remind them all the time that I own the place.

YENS. I used to own the place. It is lovely. It is brick that I lay myself. It is fine wood that I nailed. It is glass and copper. You could not touch it on today's market. They do not build houses like they used to!

PETER. Leave it to him not to mention that I helped.

YENS. He helped. A little.

PETER. A little? We'll just see how little. Come on. Go. Go. Let's get this started.

(GUNNAR *exits door and* YENS *retires to his bed.*) You'll pick things up as we go along. We'll start in the morning. It's a week day and . . . you'll see. (PETER *turns upstage.*)

SCENE 2

(*The kitchen.* GUNNAR *sits at the table finishing his breakfast and reading the newspaper. Waltzes play on the radio.* PETER *enters from stairs painfully rubbing his eyes.*)

PETER. Gunnar!

GUNNAR. You're finally up. Good morning.

PETER. Turn that—! (*Crosses to radio. He turns off the radio himself.*)

PETER. (*Crosses to center table and sits.*) How do you listen to that stuff.

GUNNAR. I like it. What's a matter? Ballerinas tippy-toeing across your fevered brain?

PETER. If you're asking do I feel like hell the answers yes.

GUNNAR. What do you expect?

PETER. Thanks for the sympathy, wise-ass.

GUNNAR. (*Rises and crosses to table.*) You want some coffee?

PETER. (*Holding out his arm.*) Inject some into my veins.

GUNNAR. (*Crosses for coffee and then to the refrigerator for aspirin.*) You'll have to settle for a cup.

PETER. And some aspirin, huh? My head's falling off.

GUNNAR. (*Crosses to table.*) How do you face the day on four hours sleep?

PETER. Backside first and eyes closed. Four hours? I was that late?

(GUNNAR *shrugs.*)

PETER. (*Annoyed.*) Screw off, Gunnar. I'm a big boy now. You're not my babysitter.

GUNNAR. The money you'd owe me if I was.

PETER. Kid, be warned. You're starting to piss me off.

(*Pause.*)

GUNNAR. Want some breakfast?

PETER. No.

GUNNAR. Some toast? Some eggs, maybe?

PETER. God, no.

GUNNAR. How about some oysters on the half shell?

PETER. Ohh . . . Gunnar, I don't eat breakfast. Every morning you ask me and every morning I say no. I'll say it again. I don't eat breakfast.

GUNNAR. Used to.

PETER. What was that?

GUNNAR. Nothing. (*Crosses to door. Pause.*) Beautiful day . . . clear, hot, sunny . . . fine day for building.

PETER. Right. Oh for gods sake, Gunnar, are you trying to kill me? There's no sugar in this coffee.

GUNNAR. (*Crosses to table.*) Half a spoonful. Sugar isn't good for you.

PETER. Life isn't good for me. Pass the bowl.

GUNNAR. (*Crosses to sink and washes up.*) Your funeral.

PETER. You were up early this morning. Couldn't sleep? (*Pause.*) I heard you in the shower. Singing. You woke me up.

GUNNAR. (*Goes to the table for dish, and then to the sink.*) I like getting up early.

PETER. Since when?

GUNNAR. It makes the day longer.

PETER. Who wants a long day when you're building a house?

GUNNAR. Something going up in front of your eyes? I like it.

PETER. Make it a career why don't you.

GUNNAR. I might.

PETER. No way. He up yet?

GUNNAR. (*Crosses to table and sits in the right chair.*) His door's open. He'll hear us and come out when he's ready. Hey. You notice he's been sleeping a lot? A week and a half home and he's slept more than he usually does in a month. It's not like him. What do you think?

PETER. I think my head hurts.

GUNNAR. Goddammit! You ever think you might have a drinking problem?

PETER. Now I am pissed. What are you talking about?

GUNNAR. Lately you're hung over seven days a week.

PETER. I've never missed a day of work because of it! Stop throwing stones, Gunnar.

GUNNAR. It's not me who lives in a glass house.

PETER. You're a pain in the ass!

GUNNAR. Yeah. (*Pause.*) We're running late. (*Rises.*)

PETER. Sit down. I want to talk to you.

GUNNAR. (*Goes to stairway for boots and belt.*) Oh man, here it comes. You always want to talk to me.

PETER. Guns, what are you going to do?

GUNNAR. And always about things like that! Jesus!

PETER. You're a smart kid, a bright kid. Why keep screwing around, banging nails in a hot sun? Nobody likes building. It's ballbusting and demeaning. People look down on it. Me? I wouldn't do it if I didn't have to. It's the only thing I know and it's a little late to change. But you, you're still a kid.

GUNNAR. Where do you get this, Dad? Look at me. I haven't been a kid for a long time.

PETER. Isn't it about time for the summer job to end?

GUNNAR. (*Goes back to right chair.*) What's wrong with building? You're a builder.

PETER. You're not listening to me. Yeah, I'm a builder but that has nothing to do with you. I never got the chance to make a choice. The old man was starting out on his own. He needed some help, he asked me. But I'm not asking you. In fact, I'm telling you. Make some plans.

GUNNAR. I like what I do. (*Sits right.*) Hey! You ever notice how on one hand you tell me how great I am, on the other you pay me minimum wage?

PETER. You could be a doctor, a teacher, a lawyer. Guns, what you do in this life might as well be your name. Don't discover that too late like I did. I want your name to mean something. So?

GUNNAR. I'll think about it.

PETER. That's all I ask. For now.

(*There is a sound off stage.* YENS *rises to walker.*)

GUNNAR. (*Rises and goes for coffee.*) Somebody's up.

PETER. I hate him clinging to the stroller.

GUNNAR. You think he likes it?

PETER. Never thought I'd see him walk two steps and then have to stop and rest. It hurts me to see him dragging himself around.

GUNNAR. Sshh. Try and laugh about it.

(YENS *enters.*)

Hey, there! Ride that horse! Giddyup! Heigh-ho, Silver! Away!

YENS. Go ahead, make fun of a tired, sick old man. Leave me in my room to die of starvation and loneliness. Ungrateful bastards, after all I've done for you.

PETER. You want some help, Dad?

YENS. Help? Look at you. You feel worse than I do. How are you going to help me? Who turned off the radio? I was waiting for the news.

GUNNAR. What do you care what's happening?

PETER. Please, don't get him started.

GUNNAR. You gonna spend the day writing letters to newspapers and magazines?

YENS. You be quiet. When I see something wrong, I speak my mind on it.

GUNNAR. You're politically to the right of Atilla the Hun.

YENS. I liked Richard Nixon!

GUNNAR. (*Crosses to chair.*) You're morally to the left of Albert Schweitzer.

PETER. In other words you give shit to everybody.

YENS. And they deserve it.

PETER. My poor, aching head.

GUNNAR. How about breakfast?

YENS. Breakfast? No, you will both be late for work. Just a little prune juice. (*Sits left chair.*)

GUNNAR. (*Crosses for juice.*) Just what you need.

(PETER *reads blue prints, slumped in chair.*)

YENS. That's what I want.

GUNNAR. You already have enough gas to move a motorboat.

YENS. I've had prune juice everyday for fifty years. I'm not changing my habits now.

GUNNAR. Stop drinking it and you won't have to click-a-bump to the bathroom twelve times a night.

YENS. What's all this sudden interest in my bowel movements? I move my duff a little slow but I get to the pot and I do my business. And that's none of your business.

GUNNAR. Listen, it's my business when I wake up and hear you creeping around down here like some kind of giant turtle.

YENS. (*Giggling.*) This damn, noisy thing. I might as well wear a bell around my neck. Let everyone know the big cow is coming. Don't get old—Peter! Sit up straight. You're not on a street corner.

GUNNAR. (*Hugging him.*) I'm getting you back. When I used to work for you summers you'd give me all the backbreaking jobs while you wandered around measuring things with a ruler.

YENS. You, always babbling at the breakfast table to put off going to work.

PETER. Finished? God . . . (*Rises, crosses for boots.*)

GUNNAR. Maybe the doctor will have the results of your test when he calls today. (*Pause.*)

YENS. Bah!

GUNNAR. Come on, it's going to be good news. (*Crosses to right chair, sits.*)

PETER. (*Crosses stage right with boots and sits.*) Goddamn right—bad news they tell you in person. Those bastards'll never get you if you make sure your only contact with'm is over the phone.

YENS. I'll be outside filling my feeders. I might not hear the phone.

PETER. He'll charge extra if he has to call back.

YENS. I saw a cardinal yesterday, a female. They're not as gaily plumed as the males. The males are the color of blood. They frighten easily. The females are calm and content. The males are always excited, tearing about in all directions. Fools. Well, in all fairness, I suppose a bird is rarely born with beauty *and* brains.

PETER. As far as I'm concerned, they're all ugly, stupid, and they make a lot of noise.

YENS. They sing.

PETER. I'm going to buy cats; big, vicious, cross-eyed Siamese cats. I'm not going to feed them either. We'll see how long those birds last. Maybe we'll finally get some peace around here. (*Crosses for coffee.*)

YENS. You used to love birds. You're both going to be late for work.

PETER. I'm the boss. I can't be late for work. Work doesn't start till I get there.

YENS. You're staying home because of me. I won't have it.

PETER. (*Crosses to table, sits center chair.*) I'm staying home because I want to.

YENS. You have your lives to live. I'm a burden. I think I should be sent to a home for the aged.

GUNNAR. Who'd have you? You'd be attacking the spinsters in their beds.

YENS. They're like summer camp, you know. Arts and crafts, bingo, ice cream. I never went to summer camp. Medicare would cover it.

PETER. Only if the patient is kept on I.V. and medication is administered by injection.

YENS. Bastards! You looked into it already? Behind my back!?

PETER. Dad, we were worried about you for awhile. We explored possibilities.

YENS. I think you should send me.

PETER. Forget it.

YENS. I am a burden.

GUNNAR. Needles, Yens. Big hollow tubes in your arms.

YENS. Peter, is my grandson teasing me?

GUNNAR. Needles as big as tenpenny nails. Tubes as thick as sausage links.

YENS. Son of a bitch! (GUNNAR *laughs, crosses to stage right chair, puts on boots triumphantly.*) Don't laugh at your grandfather. Go to work, the both of you, you lazy bums.

PETER. It's time. Come on, Gunnar.

YENS. You're going? So soon? Peter, is the work going well? If you need any help just ask me.

PETER. The work is fair, Dad.

YENS. People are building?

PETER. Well, it's kind of tight. But you know the condominiums over on the north side of town? They want us for the finishing work and there was mention of a maintenance contract.

YENS. No homes?

PETER. (*Crosses to stairwell for tool belt.*) Who can afford one, Dad?

YENS. Yes. Condominiums, developments where houses look like they came from cookie molds. No one cares if the bones are shoddy as long as the facade is showy and it's no more than ten minutes to the freeway.

PETER. We'll get by. Come on, Guns.

YENS. Peter? Wait. Friends visited while I was in the hospital. They told me something.

PETER. What did they tell you?

YENS. That people don't like to work with you in the afternoon. You drink too much at lunch.

PETER. (*Crossing stage right.*) *Some* friends, Dad.

YENS. The hell with them, Peter. They don't want to do business with us, the hell with them. But don't drink on the job. You will lose fingernails to hammers and hands to Skilsaws. I've seen it happen.

PETER. (*Goes to table.*) Dad, I could build a goddam house in my sleep. Shit! (*Pause.*) I have to go. I have four guys waiting for me who don't know plywood from peanut butter. Gunnar, get your ass in gear. (*He exits. Kitchen door with blue prints.*)

GUNNAR. Don't you worry about him. You have a good day. And listen, I care about fine homes. I'm going to build them some day.

YENS. I didn't mean to upset him. He's dissatisfied with the way the work is going, isn't he?

GUNNAR. (*Crosses left of* YENS.) Times are tight. You take what you can get.

YENS. Sometimes I think times haven't changed, expectations have. Once it was so simple. (GUNNAR *crouches.*) You took care of your family, you put food on the table. You weren't wealthy but you didn't expect to be. You had enough, and your home was filled with laughter. It was easy to be happy.

GUNNAR. It's different now, Yens.

YENS. They keep us alive too long. I could feed the family for a week on five dollars, Gunnar. Lean, red ground beef was only twelve cents a pound. Bacon, butter, bread, eggs, chicken, cheese and apples. We Danes were very big on apples, Gunnar. They made the hair blond, the teeth white, the health good. We were strong men. We worked on the homes ten, twelve hours a day. We were proud of our work. Homes— homes that families would live in. They've torn down so many of my homes to make shopping malls, to make apartment buildings. I didn't change with the times and it hurt us. All I have left to give you is my pride. Have a good day.

GUNNAR. You, too.

(GUNNAR *stands, crosses stage right for tool belt and exits kitchen door.* YENS *pauses, takes newspaper and exits kitchen door.*)

SCENE 3

(*The kitchen. Evening.* PETER *enters kitchen door with a six pack beer in hand.*)

PETER. Christ what a day! There is no moisture left in my body. (*Pause.*) *That meddling old bitch.* (*Pause.*) You want another beer?

(GUNNAR *enters kitchen, and sits in chair stage right.*)

GUNNAR. I'm fine. (PETER *cracks another can of beer, guzzles it.*) I get headaches when I drink it too fast.

PETER. (*Sitting center chair.*) Lightweight.

(And as PETER *sits,* YENS *enters with cane, birdhouse and crosses between stage right chair and center.)*

YENS. You're home. You didn't call for me?

GUNNAR. We thought we'd try to sneak in a moment's peace. *(Grinning.)* How you doing?

YENS. You. I'm fine . . . fine. I was looking for a spot to put my new birdhouse. How was the work today?

PETER. Miserable. Christ, look at my hands. Roofing, I hate roofing. The woman of the house, Dad, she had me climbing up and down the ladder all day long.

GUNNAR. She wanted to use the phone.

PETER. What were we supposed to use? Elmer's glue? A roof needs nails, nails need to be hammered, hammering makes noise. Meddling old biddy.

GUNNAR. She didn't like us drinking.

PETER. Beer is not drinking! It was a hundred degrees up there. We were risking sunstroke. I'll be damned if I know why we do it.

YENS. Because we like it.

PETER. You like it. I don't like it.

YENS. You used to like it.

PETER. Get out of building, Guns. It's a losing battle.

GUNNAR. *(Crosses to refrigerator for beer.)* I like what I'm doing.

PETER. Condominiums? Maintenance contracts? There's no future in this business.

GUNNAR. I don't care.

PETER. You goddam better start caring!

GUNNAR. *(Crosses to stage right chair.)* I don't! Jesus, Yens carries on about the past, you bitch about the present, I'm supposed to worry about the future. Just get off my case.

PETER. What's the matter with kids today, huh, Dad? I knew what I wanted to be. Everything! You picked a mountain, you went for it. Kids today, gangrene of the ambition. For christ's sake, Gunnar, I want you to be what I'm not! A success!

GUNNAR. Yeah, well, I don't know what that is! Money? Prestige? Selfworth? Maybe once I thought about that. I changed, all right? I changed.

PETER. Listen, don't you ever wake up in the morning and wonder if this is going to be the day that changes your whole life? Huh!? A certain wind is gonna like, sweep you up and . . . and set you down and nothing is gonna be the same again!?

GUNNAR. Seems to me we already had that day. We didn't like it much.

PETER. I thought you were going to unload the truck.

GUNNAR. Yeah.

(GUNNAR *exits by kitchen door. Pause.* YENS *sits right of table, birdhouse on table.*)

YENS. Maintenance contracts. We're becoming janitors. Those condominiums? Orchards once. In the fall laden with fruit . . . Condominiums. They'll sell for forty thousand and in two years they'll go for eighty. We should buy one.

PETER. With what?

(YENS *suddenly clutches in pain.*)

PETER. Dad, are you all right?

(YENS *waves him away, nodding his head. Pause.*)

YENS. Peter, would you ever sell our home?

PETER. What? Where did this come from?

YENS. It would buy a lot of condominiums.

PETER. Yeah. It would. It's occurred to me once or twice. (*Pause.*) Aaahh, I dunno. Lots of memories in this dump.

YENS. In every room. Peter, I love our home but if you ever wanted to sell it . . . for some reason . . . I would understand. I'll be gone soon and—

PETER. Jesus Christ, where do you get this stuff? I'm not going to sell the house. Who the hell'd buy it? You did such a good job on it you priced it right out of the market. (*He rises and crosses to stairs.*) God almighty, I smell like a locker room. I gotta get out of these clothes. You gone? You're gonna outlive us all. (*And he starts to exit.*)

YENS. (*Rising.*) Peter? Wait, wait.

(PETER *crosses to left of table and sits.*)

The nurse the town sends by every other day? She came yesterday. You should meet her. She says she knows you from high school, that she thought you were handsome. And you were, still are for such a foolish bastard. Her name is Betsy Simmons.

PETER. I don't know her.

YENS. She's a fine looking woman. Divorced too. With three daughters.

PETER. How do you know all this?

YENS. She told me. People tell old farts everything. If I was your age I'd take advantage of Betsy Simmons. She's very well spoken and she has a fine Danish bosom. I press against it when she takes my pulse. Interested?

PETER. No.

YENS. She didn't say you were merely handsome. She said she thought you were gorgeous.

PETER. I was. Big deal. That and fifteen bucks'll get me a new hammer.

YENS. You *were* gorgeous. Fine looking specimens of manhood; all of us. It's the Viking blood.

PETER. Goodlooking guys, Vikings . . . Jesus, Yens. Women should be born goodlooking. Men should be born with either money, brains or balls.

YENS. What were you born with? An attractive, available woman and you sit around on your duff.

PETER. It's the Viking blood, cold stuff. (*He rises.*)

YENS. (*Snorting with disgust.*) Bah. Where are you going?

PETER. (*Crosses to stairs with belt and beer.*) To take a shower.

YENS. Good! You, you smell like a locker room!

PETER. (*Returning.*) Don't try to set me up with women. Dad? Don't.

(PETER *exits. Upstairs.* YENS *sits center chair and sands his birdhouse.* GUNNAR *enters.*)

GUNNAR. You can't bear to think of anything without a home, can you? Birdhouses.

YENS. It's a hobby.

GUNNAR. (*Sitting stage right, takes off his boots.*) What's this one going to be? The Conbird Hilton? Remember how Mom used to put out seed and suet? The squirrels stole it till Dad put out peanut butter crackers for them. You do it all now.

YENS. It makes the birds sing.

GUNNAR. Mom loved those birds.

YENS. Your father used to. (*Pause.*) Isn't it an evening? The birds . . .

GUNNAR. You didn't like the hospital much, did you?

YENS. That damn place. They made me use a bedpan. Can you imagine? I told them I'd rather be dead than shit in something the size of a coffee pot. They wouldn't listen.

GUNNAR. They must have been glad to get rid of you.

YENS. Yes, I kept sticking their oral thermometers up my you-know-where. It ruins them. When I was a child no one put a thermometer under the tongue.

GUNNAR. (*Crosses to door to put boots outside.*) Sounds pretty anal.

YENS. It was a big pain in the fanny, if that's what you mean. Oh! A goldfinch. They like the thistle. The work was difficult today?

GUNNAR. It was pretty hot.

YENS. Your father came home with you. That's good. He didn't stop off to drink.

GUNNAR. (*Crosses to sink and washes his hands.*) He wanted to. We really were on the verge of tying the lady of the house to the chimney. (*Crosses right of table and sits.*)

YENS. Just like his mother. Never any patience with fools.

GUNNAR. It was the roofing. Nobody likes it. He sees me up there and he says it makes him want to cry with disgust. I don't mind it. I pull on some old basketball knee pads and it's not so bad.

YENS. We loved watching you play basketball in high school. We never missed a game.

GUNNAR. Come on, Yens.

YENS. You were a star. A Viking.

GUNNAR. I was a guard.

YENS. Remember the cheers? Larsen, Larsen, he's our man! If he can't do it . . . who did it after that, Gunnar?

GUNNAR. Gillespie.

YENS. That one, hands like sheetrock. Larsen, Larsen, he's our man. If he can't do it, no one can! Oh . . . (YENS *flinches in pain.*)

GUNNAR. Hey!

YENS. No, no, I'm fine. I haven't been taking my medication. It's useless anyway. It makes me foggy. Some one speaks and it might as well be the radio in another room. What's a little discomfort if I can keep my few wits about me. I need my wits. I have to keep an eye out for you and your father.

GUNNAR. Listen to you! You have to watch out for me?

YENS. You'd lose your head if it wasn't attached.

GUNNAR. I'll know where to look if I can't find the thermometer. (GUNNAR *rises, takes birdhouse to stairwell.*)

YENS. Touche. (*Pause.*) Gunnar, I heard you and your father talking this morning. He want to know what your plans are.

GUNNAR. Yeah.

YENS. What are they?

GUNNAR. Aw Yens, not you too.

YENS. No! I'm too old to lecture. I just want you to know that I think you're a young man of many talents and much promise. What ever you decide to do, you'll do well. Remember, you're a Viking. Imagine them . . . in a tiny ship, in the middle of the ocean, lost, no idea in which direction to go. Know what they did? They found land.

GUNNAR. Land, huh. You. (*Crosses for glass of water.*)

YENS. And you! (GUNNAR *crosses right of* YENS. *Pause.* YENS *takes pills.*)

GUNNAR. So tell me, what did the doctor say when he called today?

YENS. Did the doctor call? I must have been asleep.

GUNNAR. Oh.

YENS. He called. We talked.

GUNNAR. I know. I was in touch with him too.

YENS. What did he say?

GUNNAR. Same thing he told you.

YENS. Damn! I told him not to. Does Peter know? Good. Let me tell him. Spreading. (GUNNAR *sits.*) What an awful word. Rashes spread. Spills spread.

GUNNAR. It's Mom all over again.

YENS. No. She was young, it was a tragedy. Me, I'm an old house. Parts of me are wearing out. You will let me go, Gunnar. No helplessness. Leave me my pride.

GUNNAR. You. Pride? How can you have any pride? You voted for Richard Nixon. Twice.

YENS. Don't get me started! That man, he broke my heart. And then we lost John Wayne. They keep us alive too long, Gunnar.

GUNNAR. Maybe so. How you doing. Can I get you anything else?

YENS. Yes. Some good Danish cherry liqueur. (GUNNAR *rises and crosses to stage right counter.*) This percodan's useless. I understand it's artificial, a synthetic base.

GUNNAR. Nothing's natural anymore.

YENS. Yes, preservatives in everything.

GUNNAR. (*Returning with liqueur.*) Complain, complain.

YENS. Yes, how boring we old farts are. We complain, we moan and we rehash old stories.

GUNNAR. (*Sits.*) I like your stories, Yens.

YENS. I'm glad. Reminiscing is a large part of what I have left. I remind myself that my years have been fine and full. And yet . . . When I think of the things that have happened to me, wonderful things and some sad things too, sometimes it seems as if they never happened at all. I know they did. I was there. But there are moments when I wonder, all the pictures in my head, did I make them up? Are they real? Or have I been sitting here always.

GUNNAR. (*Softly.*) Yens? Yens, are you all right?

YENS. My hands are cold. Spreading. Oh well. Better me than you.

GUNNAR. You!

YENS. You!

(GUNNAR *crosses to family room.* YENS *crosses to bedroom.*)

SCENE 4

(The family room. Bookcases. Shelves lined with basket-
ball trophies, several game balls. There is a sewing
machine in one corner. GUNNAR *dozes on a sofa.*
PETER *comes down stairs, checks on* YENS *who*
is sleeping then crosses to family room.)

PETER. Hey. Hey!

GUNNAR. (*Sitting up.*) Huh? What? (*Pause.*) I fell
asleep. I'm pooped.

PETER. You oughta go upstairs to bed.

GUNNAR. It's better to sleep down here in case
Yens needs me.

PETER. It was hot today, huh? Yeah. My hands. Still
dirty. From the tar paper. It's oil base, you know. Won't
wash off.

GUNNAR. You notice how good I'm getting at banging roofing nails. Boom, boom and it's in.

PETER. Boom-boom is one boom less then amateur,
kid. When you can set a nail with one shot tell me
about it.

GUNNAR. Like you?

PETER. Yeah, like me. (*Pause, trying to stretch his*
spine.) My back's killing me. It's being on the roof, the
incline, y'know? On your knees, bent forward, I hate it.
I wouldn't take a dump in such a position. Days like
this I wonder if I died and gone to hell.

GUNNAR. It wasn't so bad.

PETER. Sure, that's why you're falling asleep at eight
o'clock. Christ, my head's still swimming from the
smell of melting tar. I'm seeing large colored spots in
the air.

GUNNAR. Some guys I know pay big money to do
that.

PETER. You're funny. It's lousy being a carpenter. You realize the world is built with cheap plywood. Most of it in need of covering.

GUNNAR. I think I'll call it a night now, you don't mind.

PETER. I won't let you spend the rest of your life doing that, kid.

GUNNAR. Yeah, yeah.

PETER. (*Crosses to shelves.*) All these trophies. How come you never play anymore?

GUNNAR. I dunno.

PETER. You never lose the touch, you know. I bet you could still hit eight out of ten from around the key.

GUNNAR. No way.

PETER. (*Picking up a game ball.*) High scorer in the division championships. Thirtyseven points. The game ball. Man, you were good.

GUNNAR. You were a good coach, Dad.

PETER. (*Tosses ball to* GUNNAR.) Yeah, I was.

GUNNAR. And I had a real fine cheerleader.

PETER. Yeah. Where is he, I'd ask. Dinner's on the table and getting cold. Down at the park playing your Mom would say. Basketball. Let him be late. I can warm his up. If you're so worried, go down and get him. But don't you start playing too. You don't have an excuse. Your Mom knew me too well. (*He picks up a picture from the shelf.*)

PETER. I've always liked this picture. You remember what she was laughing about? Who knows. (*Pause.*) Hey, I remember her sitting right here, tailoring your uniforms so they fit just so, huh?

GUNNAR. I was a fashionplate.

PETER. You were terrific is what you were. When she was stuck in that hospital room we listened to every game on the radio. (*He picks up a large trophy.*) And this game, oh, was it important to her. She'd be out, you know, and she'd come around for a moment and she'd ask if you were doing well. Great, I'd say. And she'd nod and smile before she fell back to sleep. You made her very proud, kid. You know . . . you should have taken that scholarship. Your Mom and I, we didn't get to college and she would have liked it if you had. It would have upset her that you quit.

GUNNAR. (*Rises.*) Maybe. (*Crosses to sewing machine.*) We ought to sell this old thing. None of us even know how to use it. We could get some new tools.

PETER. It was your Mom's. We don't sell it.

GUNNAR. Whatever you say. But man, this room's a mausoleum. I just realized. (*Pause.*) I should have been there, Dad.

PETER. It was such a big game, kid.

GUNNAR. Big game, small game, it was just a game. There was no fun left in it after that.

PETER. Well, you didn't have to keep playing but you still could have gone to college. I would have taken care of it somehow. I should have made you. You weren't in any great shape, none of us were, but I should have made you. You wouldn't still be wasting your time if I had.

GUNNAR. (*Crosses to couch and sits.*) You know, if I had a choice between you yelling at me or making me feel guilty, I'd take the yelling any time.

PETER. (*Pause, crosses left.*) She wouldn't like it what you're doing with your life, Gunnar.

(*He exits left.* GUNNAR *lifts a picture from the shelf.*)

GUNNAR. Nah, she'd be pleased.

(*Putting it back, he picks up the game ball and sends it spinning into the air.*)

GUNNAR. Two!

SCENE 5

(The kitchen. YENS *and* BETSY. BETSY *takes* YENS *blood pressure.)*

YENS. My beloved Emma and I, Betsy, we disliked each other at first sight. She was from a fine family. My family were builders, proud, and yet she looked down on us. She was as stern as glass, unyielding, as humorless and cold as an ice maiden. Out of sheer spite I took it upon myself to turn her into flesh and blood. She disliked me. She distrusted me. I frightened her. But I was persistent. I went at her like a crazy man, a roaring, ranting giant buggoon. She couldn't help herself. She giggled, she guffawed. I reduced her to helpless tears. To get even, Betsy, she married me. For fifty-four years she demanded of me, insisted of me, (BETSY *crosses right.)* would settle for nothing but the best from me. *(He shudders.)* We were very happy. She woke me one night to say that her father and brother, both long dead, were in the room. You are dreaming, my Emma, go back to sleep. She was gone in the morning. I loved her too much to grieve.

BETSY. Your blood pressure is a little high, Yens.

YENS. Of course it is. That contraption had my arm squeezed so tight the blood had nowhere to go. Do you want to take my pulse? *(She does.)* You're a fine nurse, Betsy. The ones at the hospital, skin and bone.

BETSY. *(Sitting in right chair.)* I'm sure they are highly qualified nurses. And your pulse is up.

YENS. It's the only thing that is. I didn't like the doctors there either, Betsy. I didn't like them touching me. All the probing around in a person's private places. There's no dignity in being sick.

BETSY. *(Putting bag down right of chair.)* Yens, you should be in bed.

YENS. No. When I lie down, I fall asleep. And my son, Peter, he might come home for lunch today. He'd like to see you.

BETSY. I'm sure he doesn't even remember me.

YENS. Remember you? You know what he told me? He always thought that *you* were very attractive. In fact, he said he thought you were gorgeous.

BETSY. No.

YENS. And you are. Peter's a widower, you know.

BETSY. I heard.

YENS. Cancer. Such a tragedy. He's never gotten over it. He's become shy. A grown man, but it's true. He's like a bird. He starts at the slightest threat. You know what? You and my son, Peter, should do something.

BETSY. I don't think so, Yens.

YENS. Just a movie, a chocolate sundae. No funny business. Or at least not enough to mention.

BETSY. I don't think I'd be very good at a blind date.

YENS. Who's blind? You both remember what each other looks like. You young people. You're shy like birds.

BETSY. Oh, you be quiet! (*Pause.*) He really remembered me as attractive?

YENS. A movie, Betsy? A chocolate sundae? If only I could take you for one myself.

BETSY. (*Rising.*) When you're better. Right now you're getting into bed. If you don't take care of yourself, you'll wind up in the hospital again. Let me help you.

YENS. You can't tell it to look at me but I was the image of my son once. And before that just like my grandson. Thick hair, clear eyes, strong.

BETSY. You can tell, Yens.

YENS. (*Rising.*) Do you think? Sometimes when I'm alone, I raise my arm and I look at it. I see that the muscle is gone and that the skin hangs loose from the bone . . . it doesn't bother me that much, you cannot stay young forever. But it does not seem fair that years from now, when you all think of me, the picture you'll carry is that of me dying rather then that of me living. That doesn't seem fair at all.

(*They move to the bedroom.* PETER *and* GUNNAR *enter.*)

GUNNAR. We're home. Yens?

PETER. (*Crosses to refrigerator for beer.*) Dad? Lunchtime. What are you in the mood for? Whose car is that outside? Dad?

(BETSY *enters.*)

BETSY. He's resting. Hello, Peter.

PETER. (*Pause.*) Betsy Murray.

BETSY. Simmons now. Hello.

GUNNAR. (*Crosses to* BETSY.) Hi.

PETER. (*Crosses right.*) Oh, this is my son, Gunnar. Guns, Betsy was on the cheerleading squad with your mother. She was one of those girls who didn't know a touchdown from a homerun.

(GUNNAR *pushes left chair in, crosses to sink.*)

BETSY. I just screamed when the other girls did. You, you teased me unmercifully.

PETER. Yeah, I did.

BETSY. I was so sorry to hear about . . .

PETER. It's been awhile. Look at you, you haven't changed at bit.

BETSY. Yes, I have.

PETER. (*With clumsy cheerleading gestures.*) Rah! Rah! Rah! Hold that line! Hold that . . . You were so funny! You were . . . (*Suddenly selfconscious in front of* GUNNAR.) Uh, how's Yens doing? He driving you crazy with his unending talk?

BETSY. He does tell stories.

GUNNAR. Hey, that's a Viking tradition. (*Pause.*) Sort of.

BETSY. I'm running a bit late today. My car broke down. They had to send someone to fix it.

GUNNAR. That's yours out there?

BETSY. It comes with the job. It's a lemon. I'm constantly getting stranded. I think Yens is running a slight fever. I'm taking his temperature. I better check on him. It's awfully good to see you. (*She exits to bedroom.*)

GUNNAR. Hey, Don Juan, I had better lines in grade school.

PETER. Mind your own business, Gunnar. I didn't know what to say . . .

GUNNAR. Ask her if she wants to go to bed with you.

PETER. Knock it off.

GUNNAR. (*Beginning to exit left.*) I'll ask her. Hey, you want to sleep with my father?

PETER. Hey!

GUNNAR. You got him lit up like a pinball machine.

PETER. (*Crosses to* GUNNAR.) Goddammit, stop that.

GUNNAR. Can't take the heat, huh?

PETER. Some things you don't kid about.

(BETSY *enters.*)

BETSY. He's not hungry and I've lost my thermometer. (*Crosses to bag; looking.*)

GUNNAR. I'll say hello to Yens. (*Crosses to bedroom and joins* YENS *on bed. Pause.*)

BETSY. It really is very good to see you, Peter.

PETER. You too. You want some, uh . . . a beer? Can I get you a beer?

BETSY. I think I'll stick to coffee. I carry a thermos of it everywhere. Would you like some?

PETER. Sure. I'll get some cups. (*Crosses to cups.*) Christ, look at my hands. I was fuckin' around with—

(*Sits left chair.*) I was working with fiberglass insulation this morning.

BETSY. Oh my.

PETER. Yeah. Horrible stuff. I caught this big splinter of it here at the base of my thumb. See?

BETSY. (*Crosses to* PETER *with coffee.*) That should come out.

PETER. It's nothing.

BETSY. I'm sure it's loaded with all kinds of infection. I have a needle and tweezers in my bag.

PETER. You don't have to.

BETSY. (*Sits center with kit.*) It won't take a second.

GUNNAR. Think he's going to ask her out? He's crazy if he doesn't. She's nuts for him. You can tell.

YENS. If she has anything to say about it, he will.

GUNNAR. I'll believe it when I see it.

YENS. He's a young man. He should be going out.

GUNNAR. Young, huh? He's young enough to be out of practice.

YENS. Shush. If he had any Viking sense he'd be out with her in a minute.

GUNNAR. Viking sense! Vikings raped and pillaged. They didn't go out on dates.

(BETSY *puts on glasses.*)

PETER. Listen, my language there. Carry over from the job.

BETSY. I've heard words like that once or twice before. (BETSY *takes out needle.*) Hold still, please. I'm trying not to hurt you.

PETER. Christ, I hate needles. It runs in the family.

BETSY. It won't bother you if you don't look. Turn your head. Go on. Talk about something to keep your mind off it. Tell me about building.

YENS. That was good!

PETER. Well . . . the construction trades Yens calls them. Larsen and Son—Contractors. Fine quality homes. Except nobody wants a fine quality home these days. The interest rates on a mortgage are too high. Lumber and materials are too high. Everything is too high. Aaaaaah.

BETSY. (*Taking out tweezers.*) Sorry. I almost have it. I've had a leak in my bathroom floor for over six months now. Everytime one of my daughters takes a bath, we get a deluge over the stove. There.

(GUNNAR *leans in.*)

PETER. I didn't even feel it. You can't get it fixed? The leak?

BETSY. Not for less than an arm and a leg.

PETER. I'd just take a leg. Nice leg. (*To himself.*) Oh Jesus . . .

GUNNAR. (*Crosses to left of bed.*) Christ! A line! The old man threw her a line!

YENS. (*Sitting up.*) He's a Viking!

GUNNAR. I'll get his horned helmet out of mothballs.

BETSY. (*Crosses right.*) I want to put some disinfectant on that. (*Pause.* BETSY *sits right.*) I wondered if we might finally blunder into each other sometime. We finally did. (GUNNAR *sits on trunk.*)

PETER. Yeah, we did.

(*Pause.*)

BETSY. (*Rising.*) Well, I guess I should be—

PETER. So you're a nurse.

BETSY. Pardon?

PETER. I said you're a nurse. Dumb. Of course you're a nurse.

BETSY. Yes.

PETER. I'll be. A nurse. (*Pause.*) Like it?

BETSY. (*Sits.*) Yes. (*Pause.*) I mean, it's all right.

(*Pause.*)

PETER. How'd you get to be a nurse?

BETSY. I trained.

PETER. Oh. (*Pause.*) Where?

BETSY. Oh, in San Francisco.

PETER. Oh. (*Pause.*) That's California.

GUNNAR. No, that's Alaska. Jesus Christ, what's he thinking?

YENS. He's doing fine.

GUNNAR. Viking strategy, huh? Lull her to sleep and then attack her.

BETSY. My father nearly hit the roof having to pay for it. My brothers get an education and you get a wedding, that's what he'd say. But I kept at him, badgered him and finally he consented to my becoming a nurse. I think he hoped I'd marry a doctor. He wasn't counting on San Francisco. (*Pause.*) What about you?

YENS. Good.

GUNNAR. (*Crosses to upper right corner.*) Come on, Dad, you can do it!

PETER. I dunno . . . working with my hands . . . and then . . . well, you know.

YENS. Her bathroom floor, Peter! What are you—a carpenter or an accountant!

PETER. I appreciate what you're doing for Yens. I'd be happy to fix your floor.

YENS AND GUNNAR. (*Slapping "10"!*) Yes!

BETSY. Checking on Yens is what I'm paid to do.

PETER. I could come over and at least take a look at it.

BETSY. That would be a help.

PETER. I will then.

BETSY. When?

PETER. When's a good time?

BETSY. Oh, anytime.

YENS. Friday night for gods' sake!

PETER. Friday night?

BETSY. Fine.

PETER. It won't take long. I'll just check what I need to fix it. If you have plans you can still keep them.

BETSY. I have no plans. Do you?

PETER. No.

BETSY. I could make you dinner. Nothing fancy. A meatloaf or something.

GUNNAR. He hates meatloaf.

YENS. He hates your meatloaf.

PETER. (*Rising.*) Friday night then, I'll try and make it.

YENS. Try!?

BETSY. Friday night.

(PETER *opens door.* BETSY *and* PETER *exit.*)

YENS. Friday night, Gunnar! Lost at sea they found land!

GUNNAR. Friday night. I'll be. The old man's going out on a date.

(PETER *enters.*)

YENS. Dates. What are dates, Gunnar? Two people getting to know one another. Maybe they like what they find, maybe they don't.

(PETER *closes door behind him.*)

PETER. Oh Jesus, what have I done.

(*He exits, upstairs.*)

SCENE 6

(PETER *enters the kitchen. He is drunk.*)

PETER. Lo! Anybody home? Lo! Nobody's home . . .

(*Crosses fridge for ice and then crosses right for booze. He makes himself a drink.* YENS *with cane enters.*)

YENS. We're home. Some of us just happen to be in bed.

PETER. Ey. I wake you up? Sorry. What time is it? (PETER *turns on light.*)

YENS. Almost three. Sit down, sit down. Sit down before you fall down. What was the occasion?

(PETER *drains his drink.*)

PETER. Why do I need an occasion?

YENS. No reason.

PETER. Exactly. (*He rises. Crosses to stage right counter.*) We gotta drink 'round here? (*Pause.*) Dad, I been . . . I been thinking 'bout what you said.

YENS. What is that?

PETER. Asking someone out. I should ask someone out. (*Crosses to chair right.*) A woman maybe.

YENS. (*Sits center.*) A woman would be nice.

PETER. Yeah. 'Cept Y'know . . . The thought of it makes me nervous. Nervous? Hah! The thought of it makes me sick to my stomach, you want to know the truth. It's been such a long time. See, I been thinking . . .

YENS. You've been thinking and . . . ?

PETER. I'm a carpenter. I mean, I know that has nothing to do with nothing, but like . . . she's not going to be very impressed when I crawl around on her goddam floor!

YENS. Who?

PETER. Huh? No one. Forget it . . . I'm . . . (*Pause.*) Supposing . . .

YENS. Just supposing.

PETER. There are silences. Huge silences. I'm not going to know what to say, Dad. I'll sit there starin' at my feet. I'll . . . (*Pause.*) Dad, what if a time comes and she's expectin' me to . . .

YENS. Yes?

PETER. To kiss her. What if I'm supposed to kiss her and I can't? I don't. What if she wants to . . . oh boy . . . make love? I mean, we're both adults, Dad. She might. What if she wants to and I'm not able to. Not capable of it. Jesus Christ, I hardly remember how. (*Pause. Rises crosses right.*) O' goddam! We got a drink around here or what? (*He stumbles.*) Jesus, Dad, look at me, huh? I drink too much. The kid knows. And you, you're ashamed of me. There are just these times when I . . . I dunno, get afraid. A nothin'! It's such a goddam sick feeling, Dad. But I can't help it. I try not to think about it happening. It does. If I didn't drink I'd go at my brains with the claw end of a hammer, that's all. Let's forget it. The hell with it. One more and we'll both go to bed, huh? (*Pause.*) I miss the wife, Dad. I miss her so goddam much. She's with me all the time. I feel a breeze on my shoulder, I turn around'n expect to see her standing there. I even dream about her, Dad. We're in bed and I'm holding her and we're happy. Something changes. It's like I'm suddenly watching from a doorway. Sometimes it's like she's being . . . mounted by a huge writhing octopus. This thing caresses her body. I try to do something but I'm helpless and she opens her mouth to scream and the dream goes black and I'm helpless, Dad. I wake up and I'm crying . . . I'm crying . . .

YENS. (*Rises crosses to* PETER.) Peter, Life is one long story of loss. Children lose parents. Parents lose children. Friends lose friends and lovers lose lovers. To be afraid of that for long is to die along with them.

PETER. I know. I know that, Dad. But . . .

YENS. Keep talking, Peter. It helps to talk.

PETER. Some things you just can't talk about, Dad. Look at me now, a grown man, blubbering like a kid.

YENS. Oh Peter, my son . . .

PETER. This has not been a good week, Dad. This has not been a good week at all. (*He exits towards the stairs, pauses.*) You oughta be in bed, Dad. (*He exits upstairs.*)

(YENS *turns lights off and crosses to bedroom.*)

SCENE 7

(*The kitchen,* YENS *and* GUNNAR *play cards.*)

YENS. A dollar a point?

GUNNAR. Like living dangerously, huh?

YENS. I can afford to be generous. I never pay off when I lose.

GUNNAR. He was in the shower a long time. I think he shaved twice. You think he'd like to take along some prophelactics?

YENS. Oh, for gods' sake, play cards!

GUNNAR. Just a thought.

YENS. He's coming. Don't say a word. We don't know a thing.

(PETER *checks himself in mirror, enters in jacket and tie.*)

YENS. Well, don't you look nice. What's the occasion?

PETER. (*Crosses right. Making a drink.*) Business meeting.

GUNNAR. Smell that cologne.

PETER. I cut myself shaving.

YENS. It's fine, just fine.

GUNNAR. I put the tools you'll need in the back of your car so you won't forget.

YENS. Goddam, Gunnar! We don't know that.

GUNNAR. Shit.

PETER. How much did you two hear?

YENS. I'll knock with two.

PETER. Dad?

YENS. Oh, be quiet. Fix her bathroom floor indeed. Well, it's a start.

PETER. (*Pushing in center chair.*) She's been giving you a hand. It's the least I can do.

YENS. Like birds the both of you. Be a Viking, Peter. Be a Viking.

GUNNAR. Rape and pillage her.

(PETER *swats at* GUNNAR.)

YENS. You should wear a coat and tie more often.

GUNNAR. Dad? you look terrific.

PETER. (*Very pleased at this vote of confidence.*) Thanks. I haven't been out in . . . a long time.

YENS. Go now. Don't be late.

PETER. I look O. K.?

YENS. Like a Viking.

GUNNAR. Remember, lost at sea . . .

PETER. They found land, yeah, yeah. I bet the idiots were off course to do it. Christ, I feel like I'm sixteen. See ya. (*He exits.*)

YENS. A movie, a chocolate sundae . . . who knows. Let's play again, I cheated the last hand.

GUNNAR. Play some solitaire while I get dinner going. (*He rises. Strikes dishes to sink.*)

(*A pause.* YENS *sags weakly in his chair.*)

GUNNAR. Hey, are you all right.

YENS. Not so good.

GUNNAR. (*Crosses to* YENS.) You're hot.

YENS. Isn't that strange. I feel cold. Old age.

GUNNAR. You have an appetite?

YENS. A little. I'll eat. This is a good home, isn't it, Gunnar.

GUNNAR. (*Crosses to stage right counter for linen.*) You built it.

YENS. Your father helped. He says I always forget but I just like to tease him.

(*Pause. He shivers.* GUNNAR *watches him a moment.*)

GUNNAR. I think I might give the doctor a call.

YENS. What? No. Gunnar, I'm fine, fine. It's just drafty in here and I'm a little sleepy. It's the medication playing tricks on me. Don't worry. No fuss.

GUNNAR. (*Crosses to table.*) You. You'd fuss if we didn't fuss.

(GUNNAR *begins setting the table.*)

YENS. You're right. What's this? Linen?

GUNNAR. I thought we might eat off of Mom's good china, use the silverware instead of the stainless steel.

YENS. Is it a holiday?

GUNNAR. I thought we could pretend it's our birthday.

YENS. But Peter's not here.

GUNNAR. We're just pretending.

YENS. Is there cake?

GUNNAR. Is there cake! Sara Lee! Your favorite!

YENS. Do we have candles?

GUNNAR. Hey, do we have candles!

YENS. How many candles?

GUNNAR. How many you want?

YENS. One for each of us.

(*Getting the cake from the icebox where it is hidden, candles in place.*)

GUNNAR. Three of them it is!

YENS. How wonderful! Let's have it now shall we?

GUNNAR. (*Putting the cake out of reach.*) Dinner first. You should try and eat.

YENS. Oh, let us have cake, Gunnar. Let us have a holiday. Bring on the birthday candles and wishes, that's the medication I want. I want to overdose on it. Holidays always make you well.

GUNNAR. (*Presenting each.*) We have cake! And candles! And we have Danish butter cookies! And we have Danish vanilla ice cream! Much better than the French. And Danish beer! And Danish cheese! And

Danish crackers! And last but not least, on the radio
we have . . . (*Crosses to radio turns it on.*) Danish
waltzes.

(*There is soft music.*)

YENS. (*Swaying.*) It's Copenhagen. Oh Gunnar, the
littlest mermaid is in the harbor weeping.

GUNNAR. (*Opening beer.*) Why is she weeping?

YENS. She has lost her love. She cannot follow him.
That's what the story says. I prefer to think she weeps
because we left her. She must have known we would
not return. I meant to. So much happened. Tillykke
Med Fodsendagen.

GUNNAR. (*Lights candles and sits.*) Happy Birthday
to you.

(*They toast each other.*)

YENS. Sa ma du lieve helt antid. Du har vaerte min
meste.

GUNNAR. Now you lost me. What does that mean?

YENS. You must live to the fullest forever. You have
been my most precious gift.

GUNNAR. Let's blow out the candles and make a wish.
Ready? Go.

(*They blow out the candles.*)

END OF ACT 1

ACT II

SCENE 1

(*The kitchen.* YENS *enters left.* GUNNAR *is playing solitaire. There is a noise offstage.*)

GUNNAR. Is that you, Dad?

PETER. (*Entering.*) What are you doing up?

GUNNAR. Beating the house at solitaire. By cheating. How'd it go?

PETER. (*Putting coat on center chair.*) You should be in bed.

GUNNAR. I'm getting ready to call it a night. You have a good time?

PETER. I'm going to bed. G'night.

(He turns, stumbles, falls against fridge.)

PETER. What are you looking at? Goddammit, Gunnar, why aren't you in bed? Alright, I had a little too much to drink.

GUNNAR. (*Rising.*) I'm gonna make you some coffee.

PETER. I don't want any goddam coffee. I can't drink the stuff without sugar. Goddam sugar! It's no goddam good for you.

GUNNAR. Booze is?

PETER. Oh, shit, here it comes. Fingers to hammers and hands to skilsaws. Christ Almighty. If you're going to act like some prissy-faced housewife, leave me alone. (*Crosses stage right to make drink.*)

GUNNAR. (*Crosses to* PETER.) What's her ceiling need, huh? Some boards? Some caulking? I'll be glad to help.

PETER. (*Crosses for ice.*) I don't want any help.

GUNNAR. How was dinner? You hungry? I'll make you a sandwich.

PETER. (*Crosses to stairwell.*) I don't want any goddam—will you go to bed? (*Pause.*) What kind of sandwich?

GUNNAR. How about P. B. and J.?

PETER. (*Crosses downstage.*) Peanut butter. My life's half over and I'm still eating peanut butter. Just go to bed. (*Sits left chair. Pause.*) Goddammit, go to bed!

GUNNAR. You're going to wake Yens up.

PETER. He's probably eavesdropping already and if he isn't, it's time for him to drag his ass to the toilet anyway. You want some prune juice, Dad? (*Pause.*) I wanted it to go well, Guns. She had on a new pair of slacks and her hair was . . . She looked terrific. I didn't go in. I couldn't get any further than looking through the kitchen door. Your old man chickened out, Guns. He chickened out. (*Pause.*) What's this?

GUNNAR. (*Takes cake to counter.*) Birthday cake. We were pretending.

PETER. Lot of good that does.

GUNNAR. You should have gone in, Dad.

PETER. I know. I got there and all I could do was watch for awhile like some kind of peeping tom. I stopped for a few drinks along the way and I was half in the bag. She would have taken one look at me and slammed the door in my face.

GUNNAR. No, she wouldn't have.

PETER. Gunnar, she was . . . she was wearing a silk blouse for chrissake!

GUNNAR. Call her.

PETER. Come off it. It must be two in the morning.

GUNNAR. Make an excuse. Make a joke. You gotta do something!

PETER. Let's drop it.

GUNNAR. You could tell her that—

PETER. Goddam, drop it! Don't give me advice. Don't lecture me. I don't find it appropriate. I'm the father here. I tried. I couldn't do it. (*Crosses to sink with glass.*) I should have known. I'm going to bed.

GUNNAR. Why? So you can have more bad dreams? So you can yell in your sleep and wake us all up? I hear Yens creeping around down here, half the time he's not going to the bathroom, he's trying to negotiate the stairs so that he can get to you. Christ, the old lady'd die all over again if she could see what her death has done to you.

(PETER *strikes* GUNNAR.)

PETER. You, you little shit, you quit!

(YENS *wakes up and rises.*)

You had a scholarship! You were going to be somebody! It would have made me proud! But you quit!

GUNNAR. Because it was crap! Stupid, worthless crap, and I was so caught up in it, I didn't see what was going on around me. I like what I am and I like what I do. You don't so you can't understand that.

(*A long, hostile silence.*)

PETER. I want you out of the house by the middle of next month. And you're off the job as of right now. You're fired. Don't report on Monday. Somebody else will be in your place.

GUNNAR. Why?

PETER. Because you're my son and I don't want to see you carrying tarpaper and shingles up ladders. I don't want to see you washing shit and grime off your hands at the end of each day. You're better than that.

GUNNAR. Why are you throwing me out of the house?

PETER. I don't want you playing nursemaid to a dying old man. I don't want you playing mommy to a middle-aged one. You need some money, you let me know. (*He sits down left.*)

GUNNAR. Money. No, I don't need any money.

(GUNNAR *exits. Silence.* PETER *rises, puts on jacket and crosses to door.* YENS *enters with walker.*)

YENS. Well. Aren't you a fool.

PETER. He's my son. I don't want him to end up like me. He's got to get moving. He'll sit around here thinking, someday this, someday that . . . Well, someday finally gets here and it's no different. It's like any other. Unless . . . you make someday now. I love him enough to do that for him.

YENS. Where are you going?

PETER. Out. (*Opens door.*) To a bar. Any objection?

YENS. Yes. A Viking should drink for joy.

PETER. A Viking . . . I'm no Viking. The only Vikings I know about are football players.

YENS. (*Crosses to* PETER.) Tell me about your date before you storm out.

PETER. You know exactly how it went. Every damn thing that goes on in this house you know about. You eavesdrop and Gunnar makes coffee.

YENS. You'd better start getting used to instant, hadn't you?

PETER. (*Crosses to* YENS.) Goddammit, some things around here do not concern you.

YENS. Of course they do.

PETER. Stop interfering.

YENS. And what if I don't? Will you throw me out too?

PETER. It's not a bad idea.

YENS. I'll leave then.

PETER. (*Pause.*) I didn't mean that. What I did with Gunnar, I did for his own good.

YENS. If you believe that.

PETER. (*Crosses stage right.*) I did what needed to be done.

YENS. No.

PETER. Yes. He hates what he's doing.

YENS. You hate it. He loves it.

PETER. He holds onto this job because since his mother died he seems to need some kind of security—

YENS. Horseshit.

PETER. Dad, he's gotta sink or swim.

YENS. He's a sailor now?

PETER. That's what you call us with your Viking shit.

YENS. You took his work, Peter. He'll find more. Probably hammering nails and sawing boards. That's what he likes to do. But why did you take away his home?

PETER. (*Crosses to right chair and sits.*) It's time.

YENS. (*Crosses to left chair.*) No. It's never time. People having no one to share their meals with? It's never time for that.

PETER. Christ! It's for his own good. The kid should be on his own.

YENS. Peter! Your son has been on his own since his mother died and you don't even know it. It is you who will be on your own. You and instant coffee. Alone!

PETER. Alone!? No, never alone. You'll be right there like a goddam backseat driver giving your unwanted opinion on everything I do.

YENS. Not for long, Peter.

PETER. What?

YENS. I'm dying. There is cancer inside. The doctor said.

PETER. No! Not you too. Oh god . . . god.

YENS. Yes, there is a god. I believe that. But belief is not my Aladdin's lamp and God is not my genie. They say the Viking god Odin hung on a barren tree for seven days and seven nights, dying each moment so he could learn what it's like to live. Having endured, he expects us to endure. Having endured, he rarely listens when you call his name. I've had my say. Go to your bar. Drink. I'll be in my room mourning for you. (*He crosses to bedroom and sits on bed. Pause.*)

SCENE 2

(*The bedroom.* GUNNAR *and* YENS. GUNNAR *sits center of* YENS.)

YENS. Your father's taking me for a ride in the car today. To cheer me up. He thinks I'm miserable. And I am. Your father's been in such a foul mood he'd make anybody miserable. I won't let him take me on the interstate. Insanity. I get frightened enough to piss my pants. Progress, how high you jump, how fast you go. When I'm gone will there anybody left who remembers what it is like to walk. (*Pause.*) You're not listening. What are you thinking about.

GUNNAR. I dunno. Things.

YENS. I'm glad we old farts don't think. We get senile instead.

GUNNAR. Dad, I remember when he came home from building, judging how well the day's work had gone by how sweaty and tired he was.

YENS. Yes.

GUNNAR. Somehow he'd picked up a song during the course of the day, a waltz maybe, and he'd dance Mom around the kitchen to it. He'd sweep me up and give me a toss towards the ceiling. I'd shriek. I'd want him to do it again. I knew he wouldn't drop me. He'd never drop me. Guess what I'm going to be when I grow up. It changed each day of the week back then. I'm going to be a . . . I dunno. Always something wonderful and important so he'd think I was wonderful and important. But I knew inside. I wanted to be what he was, a builder. I mean, I thought he was the most successful man in the world. And now . . . I guess even the most successful man, if he spends too many nights in the kitchen alone, must start to wonder if his life isn't like a bad house . . . showy facade, shoddy bones; too goddam close to the freeway.

YENS. I miss you. You tease me dreadfully but I miss you. Come back home.

GUNNAR. Nah.

YENS. So stubborn. Your father wants you to. He thought he was throwing out his son the bum. He didn't realize you are also his best friend. There's a difference.

GUNNAR. Is there, Yens?

YENS. Mmmm?

GUNNAR. Maybe he's right. Maybe I am wasting my time, I dunno. I could do other things. I mean, maybe I don't *like* building as much as I just *don't mind* it, huh? And maybe I never got out on my own cause staying here seemed like the thing I *should* do. It's all gotten confused lately.

YENS. Yes. This is something I can't help you with. We come from a family of builders. It never occurred to me to search elsewhere. More important, it wasn't expected of me. It's different now.

GUNNAR. Yeah. So what do I do?

YENS. Choose, then choose again. Remember! Lost at sea?

GUNNAR. Yeah, we found land.

YENS. Yes, because we're Vikings!

GUNNAR. Yes, with a trace of Spaniard.

YENS. Never!

GUNNAR. What about that certain Spanish sailor who took a left at the littlest mermaid?

YENS. What about him?

GUNNAR. Well, he was good looking and he liked blondes . . .

YENS. The bastard.

GUNNAR. And before he tacked his way back to Madrid, he impregnated quite a few of them.

YENS. Your great-great-grandmother was an innocent Viking maiden, Gunnar!

GUNNAR. You can't take it, us being part Spanish!

YENS. Don't make fun of your grandfather! Here I am, as good as dead and you try to hurry me along.

GUNNAR. If I had my way I'd pack you in a rowboat and send you out to sea right this minute!

YENS. Now you're talking! The Vikings placed their dead in long ships. Did you know that? We knew what we were doing then, great dragonheaded funeral pyres, swallowed by the ocean. I would like that.

GUNNAR. You, what do you know about long ships and the ocean? You haven't been to the beach in years.

YENS. What do I know about the ocean? What does an Italian know about spaghetti? What do the Japanese know about clock radios? We were sailors, Gunnar. I close my eyes and the ocean is this close.

GUNNAR. You're a thick headed Dane, Yens.

YENS. My father's son, father to my son, who is father to a son. You.

GUNNAR. And you. (*He rises.*) I'm going to pack some things. Talk to you in a bit. (*Crosses to right of bed.*)

YENS. You'd better.

GUNNAR. Thanks Yens.

(*He exits upstairs.* YENS *lets his shields down. He is weak and in pain.*)

YENS. (*Lying back.*) I'm not doing so well today, Emma. Not so well at all.

SCENE 3

(BETSY *and* GUNNAR *are in the kitchen.* BETSY *sits center and* GUNNAR *sits right.*)

GUNNAR. Now on the sixth day, the electricians did the wiring, the plumbers did the plumbing, and we did the interior work. Carpets were laid and furniture was moved in. And we got drunk that night, really drunk, because the work . . . was good! We were proud of it. On the seventh day we rested. Or we tried to. See, around noon the owners of the house called us up and said, Hey! What the hell kind of house is this? You put it up in a week! (BETSY *crosses to fridge. He and* BETSY *laugh,* BETSY *wincing.*)

GUNNAR. There, that's the kind of joke builders tell. (*Pause, pointing to her glass.*) More?

BETSY. No, I'm fine.

GUNNAR. I apologize for not having diet soda.

BETSY. I can tell I'm in a house without women.

GUNNAR. Homes! Homes! That's what Yens calls houses. Homes.

BETSY. (*Crosses to table with sandwich fixings.*) He's a wonderful man, your grandfather. Do you know what he told me about the other day? Norns.

GUNNAR. Oh, no.

BETSY. The Viking figures of fate. The past, the present, and the future.

GUNNAR. Sounds like this place.

BETSY. Yens says they weave. They have flax and they weave and what they weave is so fragile, a little breeze could come along and it would break—poof!— right in their fingers.

GUNNAR. Lives are what those old crones weave, Betsy. When the weaving's done, the thread is cut. (*Laughing.*) And supposedly they only have one eye between the three of them. They pass it back and forth, sharing it. That's why life is such a crazy tapestry. At any one time two out of the three weavers are groping about in the dark. (*Pause.*) The old man's an optimist. You sure you don't want some juice or something?

BETSY. No, I'm fine. It must have been very difficult for all of you when your mother passed away.

GUNNAR. Oh, yeah. My dad, he still finds it difficult.

BETSY. Yens told me he's like a bird. That made me laugh because your father seems anything but birdlike. Birds are small and fragile.

GUNNAR. People aren't?

BETSY. Oh, you'd be amazed at how tough people are. When I was working in the hospital the things I'd see. You'd be sure someone was gone for good, and then they'd pull out of it. Sometimes it seemed they just weren't ready to let go. They had unfinished business. (*Pause.*) Thank you again for the work yesterday.

GUNNAR. Hey, it was a good deal. You made me lunch.

BETSY. That's what I do. Trade meals for labor. It's not always so successful.

(*Pause.*)

GUNNAR. It was great meatloaf.

BETSY. I had some left over.

GUNNAR. It made a great sandwich.

BETSY. I'm glad. I miss seeing people eat. Really eat. My daughters don't eat. They push food around their plates. Men eat.

GUNNAR. He planned on showing. Something came up.

BETSY. Your father and mother were the most beautiful couple I have ever seen. They were . . . perfect. She looked like a young Greta Garbo and he looked like . . . you. (*Returning food to fridge.*) They were all each other wanted. The bridesmaids were all cheerleaders. We cried at the wedding. We fought for the bouquet. It's not like today. If one of my daughters ever caught a bridal bouquet, she'd drop it like a hot potato. They were the world to each other. (*Sits center.*)

GUNNAR. Yeah. (*Pause.*) My dad's upset that I don't want more from life. He doesn't like me being a carpenter.

BETSY. You're a good one.

GUNNAR. I am. And I like it, I guess. But he wanted me to go to college and I . . . well, I didn't want to go.

BETSY. Why not?

GUNNAR. (*Rises, crosses stage right.*) My mom passing away just drained all the kid stuff right out of me. I couldn't see myself shooting baskets and drinking beer with a bunch of college punks. I think I could go now but dad, he starts in on me, and the next thing you know, he has me saying I wouldn't be caught dead there in a million years. We're stubborn bastards, we Danes. (*Pause.*) That meatloaf, that sure was the best sandwich I've had in a long time.

BETSY. (*Rises, pours juice.*) You come back over any time. I'll be happy to make you another one.

GUNNAR. I guess I should get some things together.

BETSY. You wouldn't let me pay you the other day. Couldn't I at least give you something for the materials?

GUNNAR. Dad handles all the billing. Betsy . . . he could really use someone . . . my dad. You know what I mean?

BETSY. (*Crosses to bedroom, food on a tray.*) And maybe you could too, Gunnar. To make you sandwiches.

GUNNAR. I'll say goodbye before I leave.

BETSY. Good.

(GUNNAR *exits upstairs.* PETER *enters with grocery bags and crosses to table.*)

PETER. I'm home. You want lunch, Dad? Is Gunnar here? Dad? (*He puts bread on top of refrigerator.*)

BETSY. (*Entering from bedroom.*) Hello, again, Peter.

PETER. Oh, hi.

BETSY. I'm stranded again. The town car. They had to come and tow it this time. I'm making my rounds by taxi cab.

PETER. I came home to have some lunch with Yens.

BETSY. I'll tell him.

PETER. Betsy, I'd still like to do your floor for you.

BETSY. Your son came by and did it Sunday.

PETER. Gunnar did?

BETSY. Didn't he tell you?

PETER. It must have slipped my mind.

BETSY. Oh, he wouldn't accept money for the job and I'd like to at least pay for the materials. Send me a bill, would you? (*She exits.*)

(PETER *unpacks grocery bag and puts some things in refrigerator.* GUNNAR *enters from stairs with duffle bag.*)

GUNNAR. Hey.

PETER. Hey! How are you? I saw your car. I hoped you might be here.

GUNNAR. (*Crosses right.*) Just getting a few things.

PETER. Where you been the last coupla days? I've been worried sick, I don't mind telling you.

GUNNAR. You threw me out.

PETER. Not till September.

GUNNAR. (*Crosses to door.*) Then, now, what's the difference? Well, see you.

PETER. Guns? Hey, Guns, guess what? I haven't had a drink since Friday night. Yens says I look like hell. He says if he felt as bad as I look, he'd have died two months ago. Nothing but prune juice from now on. You think I can do it?

GUNNAR. If you want.

PETER. (*Displaying them.*) Hey! How about some lunch? Got some cold cuts, some rye bread, cookies—

GUNNAR. Nah, that's O.K.

PETER. Where you going?

GUNNAR. I found this little place the other afternoon. I'm taking this stuff over. And I have a buddy who wants his kitchen rebuilt. I'm going to check with him on that.

PETER. (*Putting cans in cabinet.*) You work fast.

GUNNAR. I try to.

PETER. You really like the building, don't you?

GUNNAR. Yeah.

PETER. You're good at it. I didn't know how good till we got this new guy in your place. He takes a break every five minutes and he bends more nails than he sinks. He's already asked me for a raise.

GUNNAR. Sounds like a real Spaniard.

PETER. Yeah. He is . . . a real Spaniard. (*Pause.*) Y'know, I was thinking . . .

GUNNAR. Yeah.

PETER. You sure you don't want some lunch?

GUNNAR. No, that's O.K.

PETER. Yeah. Well, kid . . . don't be a stranger.

GUNNAR. I have some more stuff to grab. I'll be by for it later.

PETER. See ya.

(GUNNAR *exits door.* PETER *stands motionless. There is a sound of* BETSY *entering.* PETER *begins to unload his bags.* BETSY *enters, her bag in hand.*)

BETSY. He's not hungry. He won't admit it but I think he's in a little pain. If it continues into the evening, I'd give the doctor a call. (*Puts bag on table, makes note in notebook.*) I'll make a point of stopping to-morrow to check on him. (*Long pause.*) I've called my cab. I'll wait outside. Have a good afternoon, Peter. (*Crosses down right.*)

PETER. (*Crosses to bedroom.*) About Friday evening—

BETSY. You don't have to explain. I misunderstood. I assumed it was going to be a social as well as a business call. Send me a bill.

PETER. No! Wait a second, you didn't misunderstand . . . I . . . Uh . . . Any coffee in your thermos?

BETSY. Yes.

PETER. Can I have some? I've been drinking nothing but instant lately. I don't like it much. I have a confession to make. I take sugar in my coffee. (*Crosses for cups center.*) It's not good for me. I take it anyway. Two huge, heaping spoonfuls, see? Look, I'm going to throw in another one for good measure. That's the nail on the coffin but it tastes good and I like it. (*Pause.*) Thank you for the coffee. Do you have to go? I want to show you something. (*He gets a highs school yearbook from the lower cabinet.*) I dug this out the other day. You're right, you have changed. Please sit, the cab will beep when he gets here. (*She sits.*) Look here's me. Just a crew cut and a big grin back then.

BETSY. (*Reading.*) In love with sports and a certain cheerleader.

PETER. And voted most—this and that—it's not important. But here, listen to this—wants to go into business with his father. Incredible. I don't remember that. Business with his . . . amazing. Hey, hold on, look at this page. Does that bring back memories?

BETSY. Oh, my God, the cheerleaders.

PETER. Here's you and here's . . .

BETSY. She was very beautiful, Peter. And sweet too.

We tried very hard to be jealous of her but it was impossible.

PETER. (*Crosses to fridge.*) I'm getting over it. It's taking time but I'm getting over it. I can hear her. 'Goddammit,' she'd say, 'pull yourself together. Shape up or ship out.' That's what she'd say. And if I'd ever stood her up, she'd have nailed my ass to the wall, no two ways about it! (*Crosses to bedroom.*) If you want to do the same, you can.

BETSY. I don't know you well enough.

PETER. Yeah, but goddam would you like to? Let me warn you, I'm no goddam first prize. I'm not—I dunno—aging gracefully. I can't talk to people anymore. It would help if I could. I can't even talk to my son, except to yell. (*Sits left chair. Pause.*) I drink too much. I'd say I was an alcoholic except I don't really like being drunk. I like being—numb. I'm trying to switch to prune juice. I don't know which takes more out of you, booze or prune juice. You're giggling.

BETSY. And why shouldn't I giggle? (*Showing him the book.*) Most charming.

PETER. Yeah. And most likely to suc—Somewhere along the line it all went wrong and if I could only figure out where and how . . . I miss her, Betsy. And yet, there are moments when I find myself acting like it was a choice she made and I resent her for leaving me alone.

BETSY. It's time for that frame of mind to end.

PETER. Yeah. (*Pause.*) Why don't we go out, you and I, on a date. Dinner? A movie, Christ, even dancing maybe. I'll show, I promise. Vikings are stern and cold but I'm part Spanish so maybe it won't be too bad. What do you say? Say something. I've run out. I'll start again from the beginning if you don't.

(*Pause.*)

BETSY. (*Looking at the yearbook.*) Best couple. I had such a crush on you. A lot of us did. You were good looking, athletic, ambitious. And in love with the prettiest girl in school. I thought I'd outgrown infatuation but there I was Friday night; changing my clothes, changing them again, cursing my hair, snapping at my daughters until they got disgusted and went off to a movie. There I was. Terrified. All the newfound confidence and selfassurance right out the window. What would the neighbors think, what if you didn't like me, good god, what if you did. What if you . . . got fresh. Do you know what I did? I drank a whole bottle of white wine. If you had come by, you would have found me . . . available.

PETER. I did show. I peeked in through the window.

BETSY. And you didn't come in?

PETER. No.

BETSY. Like a bird. (*Pause.*) My husband . . . was a surgeon, a very fine one. Did you know that? Yes. He stayed in San Francisco. The divorce was my decision. It wasn't an easy one to make. The only expectations I'd been given as a young girl were emotional ones; love a man, love a family. I'd never wanted more than that. To admit that it didn't work was to admit that I had failed. I knew that my daughters, that everyone would expect me to be strong and self-reliant. I didn't know if I was strong and self-reliant. I didn't know if I really wanted to be. (*Pause, with a smile.*) I am. And if I'm not, well . . . I don't show it. I put up a good front.

PETER. Very good.

(YENS *sits up.*)

BETSY. You're very sweet, Peter. I guess being lonely was something neither of us were prepared for.

PETER. Dinner? Dancing?

BETSY. A movie? A chocolate sundae? (*Laughing.*) Well, my floor gets fixed and I make you dinner. My

floor has been fixed. (*A horn beeps, she rises.*) Saved
by the cab! I've got to run. You'd better show this time!
I'll expect you tonight!

PETER. Tonight! (*They cross to door.*)

        (*She suddenly kisses him. She exits.*)

PETER. Thank you! Thank you!

YENS. (*Entering.*) I know. I heard.

PETER. That Gunnar. He fixed her floor for me.

(YENS *sits at the table center.* PETER *joins him right.*)

YENS. He saved your ass is what he did. (*Pause.*)
Bring him home? For me? Coax him a little, that's all
he wants. Let him decide when he leaves. (YENS *gently
takes his son's hand.*) Look at the scars. You were so
embarassed by the sixth finger. And when you had
them taken off, you were embarassed by the scars.

PETER. People would ask and I'd say I got them from
a chain saw. Look at your hands. Gnarled and cut up
and calloused. Like pieces of old wood. You have
beautiful hands, Dad.

                (*Pause.*)

YENS. You are going to see her?

PETER. Yes.

YENS. Good.

PETER. I may be a Viking but I'm not so stupid I
don't recognize land when I see it. And you're going
to have to do something for me.

YENS. What?

PETER. No more taking your pulse? I get jealous easy.

YENS. You!

PETER. You!

(*They giggle, then laugh, then bellow, slapping their
thighs, gasping for air, helpless.* YENS *stops suddenly.*)

PETER. What's the matter? What happened?

YENS. Emma. My lovely Emma.

SCENE 4

(*The family room.* GUNNAR *is putting things in a duffel bag* PETER *enters through kitchen door. Pause. Crosses to family room.*)

PETER. Hey.

GUNNAR. (*Looking up.*) Hey. How was your ride?

PETER. Huh?

GUNNAR. You and Yens go for a drive?

PETER. Uh, yeah.

GUNNAR. I'm just getting some final things.

PETER. Oh.

GUNNAR. (*Crosses to shelf.*) Can I have this picture of Mom?

PETER. Yeah. Sure. Anything you want here you . . . you take. You want the ball?

(*Pause.*)

GUNNAR. O.k. (*Crosses to bag. Pause.*) The kitchen fell through. For the money he wants to spend, I'd end up making fifteen cents an hour after expenses. He'll have to make due with what he has.

PETER. Tough everywhere.

GUNNAR. Preservatives in everything.

PETER. If you need some money . . .

GUNNAR. Yeah.

PETER. For whorehouses, beer . . . even something unimportant. Just ask.

GUNNAR. Thanks.

PETER. (*Crosses to couch, sits.*) Listen, uh . . . I want to thank *you*. For coming through for me and fixing Betsy's floor.

GUNNAR. I had the time.

PETER. You like her, Gunnar?

GUNNAR. Is it important?

PETER. Yeah. It is to me, yeah. You think your mom would like her? That matters to me too. I think she would . . . Hey, you ever consider becoming an architect? (*He rises, crosses to* GUNNAR.)

GUNNAR. What?

PETER. An architect. I was thinking, I bet between the two of us we could come up with the money to send you to school for it. And you'd be swell at it. You have the talent and the brains and—I'd bet it's make, y'know, your mom real happy—would have made. Who knows, maybe we could work on a couple of projects together. You could throw a little business my way. Would you like to be an architect?

GUNNAR. Something to think about.

PETER. Yeah, well that's all I ask. (*Crosses to upper right corner.*) Hey, did you know I was captain of my high school football team, vice-president of my class, and voted—among other things—most popular, best athlete, most charming and most likely to succeed? I was also best looking to boot.

GUNNAR. Yeah?

PETER. That's what my high school yearbook says. Know what else it says? I couldn't wait to say the hell with all of that and go into business with Yens. That was the summer we built the house, the showcase for the family business. An advertisement, this is what Yens Larsen and *Son* can do. Nothing was too good, too expensive. Everything had to fit just so. We spent a month on the kitchen alone. It was very good work we did. (*Pause. Crosses to couch.*) So, listen, you're between jobs right now, I could use some help.

GUNNAR. I dunno . . .

PETER. I'd like you to. For as long as you want. If you ever decide to go to school or try something else, fine. But it doesn't matter. Whatever makes you happy. (GUNNAR *for the first time stops packing. He is visibly moved.*)

PETER. I'd like you to come home, too. It's just an empty house without you . . . a well constructed advertisement.

GUNNAR. (*Pause.*) Thanks, Dad.

(PETER *holds out his hand, expecting a handshake hugs his father.* PETER *is at first self-conscious but then embraces back, happily, grateful.*)

PETER. I love you, kid. You're the most important thing in my life. (*They part.*) Hey, you hungry?

GUNNAR. Starving.

PETER. Let's hit the pancake joint down on Route 10. Remember that place? We used to stop there on the way home from visiting your mother.

GUNNAR. (*Grinning.*) I'm not crazy about that place. I associate it with bad news.

PETER. So do I, kid. So do I.

(*And suddenly* GUNNAR *knows what has happened.*)

GUNNAR. You have something you want to tell me?

PETER. (*Lightly.*) Yeah.

(*And* GUNNAR *knows and can feel the grief welling up inside him but he fights it down.*)

GUNNAR. (*Crosses right.*) Wait a second . . . O.K.

(*And* PETER *knows that he knows.*)

PETER. This afternoon. But it was so easy and peaceful . . . His heart. He called your grandmother's name as if she were standing there in the room, beckoning for him. There was no pain. None of those lousy needles and tubes. There was dignity.

(*Pause.*)

GUNNAR. (*Fighting tears desperately, trying to disbelieve.*) If I go in his room now . . . he'll be lying in bed, waiting for me . . . won't he? No, he won't. I'm glad we had the birthdays. Oh shit.

(GUNNAR *cries quietly.* PETER *puts his arms around his son and this time there is none of the awkwardness of the first embrace. He is a pillar of paternal*

strength, a well of comfort, the patriarch of his
family.)
PETER. It's o.k. It helps.

SCENE 5

(*The kitchen.* GUNNAR *enters from the outside. He has*
YENS'S *birdhouse. He places it on the kitchen
table.*)

(*Pause.*)

(*He enters* YENS'S *bedroom. He fluffs a pillow. He
straightens and smoothes the blankets.*)

(*He comes back into the kitchen. He goes to the radio,
clicks it on. A waltz plays. He quickly turns it off.*)

(*He sits at the table, lost in thought. He begins to sand
the birdhouse.*)

(PETER *enters down stairs in dress pants and shirt,
carrying a tie and suit coat.*)

PETER. (*Crosses to center chair, putting coat on it,
puts on tie.*) Where you been? You oughta be getting
ready.

GUNNAR. There's time.

PETER. My tie straight?

GUNNAR. Yeah.

PETER. Look at me, huh? Do I make a suit look like
khakis and a t-shirt or what?

GUNNAR. You look real fine.

PETER. Thanks. Go change, Guns.

GUNNAR. I will. (*He picks up birdhouse, takes it
outside.*)

PETER. I told Betsy we'd pick her up. You don't
mind, do you?

GUNNAR. (*Re-entering.*) No. You been seeing a lot
of her in two days.

PETER. Yeah. She's very nice.

GUNNAR. You sleeping with her?

PETER. Yeah. That's very nice too. Guns, you gonna go to the funeral looking like you been tramping through swamps?

GUNNAR. (*Crosses to counter to wipe hands on towel.*) I was filling his feeders. They didn't need much. You got to'm before me, didn't you? Awful quiet out there.

PETER. I keep expecting him to creep through the door, demanding prune juice.

GUNNAR. Speaking of which, you want a drink?

PETER. No.

GUNNAR. (*Crosses to fridge.*) I need a beer.

PETER. He wasn't afraid, Guns. He knew what was happening but was not afraid of it. That's a wonderful thing.

GUNNAR. You think he'd mind what we did?

PETER. I didn't realize the plot was so small when he insisted we put your mom there.

GUNNAR. He always said those Viking ships went down burning.

PETER. I saw the box his ashes go in. It's about so big. Fine wood, brass. It'll go right next to your grandmother. I think he'd be pleased.

(GUNNAR'S *eyes fill. He fights tears.* PETER *notices.*)

PETER. (*Crosses to mirror in stairwell straightening tie.*) Hey, Guns, we got a drink around here or what?

GUNNAR. (*Crosses to stage right counter.*) We sure do!

PETER. Make your old man one. Prune juice straight up. Hey, you want to hear something? He left this. (*Taking a paper from his jacket pocket.*) I thought I'd read it at the funeral. (*He reads.*) There comes a time. A wind blows. Nothing is the same again. Ah, but don't think you're getting rid of me that easily. Here's what

I want. No grieving, no tears, I have no stomach for funeral durges. Let's get it over with, short and quick, and then perhaps a party, a holiday. Gather family and friends together, eat, drink, tell stories, and if I should be the subject of some, better still. And listen, if you're out driving some time and you pass one of my houses, maybe you'll stop and knock on the door. If the family doesn't know who built it, you'll tell them. Ah, that crazy thickheaded bastard Yens, you'll say. He was big and strong and proud and he loved his family and his work and he never minded his own business and had no patience for those who did. He was a Viking. With a trace of Spaniard for flavor. And he was a hell of a lot of fun. And one more thing you'll do for me . . . take care of my birds.

(GUNNAR *crosses to fridge, pours juice.* PETER *sits center chair.* GUNNAR *gives him glass. Pause.*)

GUNNAR. (*Toasting.*) The sea.

PETER. Mmm?

GUNNAR. (*At center chair.*) He loved the sea and he wanted a Viking funeral. A dragon-headed ship . . . He hadn't seen the ocean in years and he still loved it. Oh, you . . . you . . .

(*Both their eyes fill. Pause.*)

PETER. (*Rising, putting on jacket.*) Well, goddammit, come on.

GUNNAR. What?

PETER. We'll goddam well take him down to the goddam ocean.

GUNNAR. What?

PETER. We'll pick up Betsy, pick up Yens and take him down to the ocean. Give a handful of him the heave-ho.

GUNNAR. Are you crazy? There'll be swimmers. Hobey-cats!

PETER. We'll time the toss.

GUNNAR. What about the relatives?

PETER. Let 'em wait. They don't want to do business with us, the hell with them.

GUNNAR. Yeah! The hell with them, they don't want to do business with us. I'll start the car. Yens! You're going to be late for your own funeral.

(GUNNAR *runs out. He re-enters.*)

GUNNAR. You.

PETER. You.

(GUNNAR *exits.*)

PETER. (*Crosses downstage.*) There comes a twilight. The cold Viking sun turns black and falls into the sea. The sea overflows its banks. The world is darkness and cold and confusion. The Viking gods march forth to do battle. The darkness consumes them and they are suffocated by its venomous breath. And yet they are victorious. There is no trumpet of defeat in their throes of death. New life is born from their struggle. There is peace. (*Pause.*) So . . . now you know. Probably more than you bargained on, huh? Well, as Gunnar said, this storytelling is a Viking tradition. *Sort of.* Me? I was overruled, two to one. (*Directing this offstage.*) Pretty goddammed slim victory if you ask me! (*There is laughter.*) Ah, enough. I have rooms to clean, houses to build. For beer and sandwiches you come back another time. (*Pause.*) It's a good house. (*Pause.*) You. You must live to the fullest forever. See ya. (*He turns to exit upstage.*)

LIGHTS OUT

MUSIC

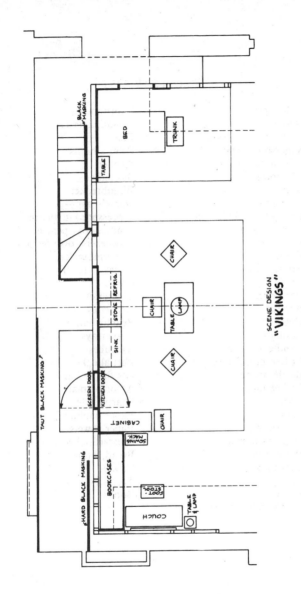

SCENE DESIGN
"VIKINGS"

PROPERTY LIST

2 Blue prints
Newspaper
Cereal bowl, spoon
Sugar bowl, spoon
2 Tool belts
G's boots
Beer
Casserole
Cake, 3 candle holders,
  cake stand
Ice cream
Cheese
Prune juice
Apple
Percodan
Aspirin
Crackers
Cookies
Candles, matches
Coffee pot, filters
Bottle opener
Coffee mugs
Glasses
Tray
Silverware
Napkins in rings
Placemats
Yearbook
Booze
Radio
Sneakers (Gunnar)

2 Birdhouses,
  sandpaper (2)
Cane
Peter's boots
Stroller
Basketball
Windbreaker
Nurse's bag—
  pressure kit, thermos,
  notebook, pen, needle,
  tweezers, disinfectant,
  thermometer,
  glasses (eye)
Cards
Cigarettes
Groceries
Peanut butter
2 Ashtrays
Ice cubes
Partial cake
G's duffle bag
Assorted plates
Sharp knife
Paper napkins
Paper towels
Mustard, cheese,
Bread, butter
Pickles
Trophies
Books
Framed photographs

FURNITURE AND DRESSING

Kitchen
table, 4 chairs, (3 at table, 1 DS edge of SR cabinet unit), sink (R), stove (C), refrigerator with cabinet unit, cabinet unit (RC) with radio, wall telephone, ceiling fixture hanging over table

Bedroom
single bed, nightstand with lamp (SR of bed), wooden chest at foot of bed, portrait over bed

Family room
sofa, footstool, cabinet w/shelves, sewing machine, trophies, books and photographs on shelves

COSTUME PLOT

Betsy: Blue uniform with identification pin
White stockings and shoes
Half slip

Gunnar: Socks
I-1 through I-4: jeans, t-shirt, sneakers (work
        shoes pre-set)
I-5: work pants, t-shirt, sneakers
I-7: jeans, sport shirt, sneakers
II-1: same as above
II-2: through II-4: jeans, work shirt, sneakers
II-5: jeans t-shirt, sneakers

Peter Socks, undershirt, watch, wedding ring
I-1 through I-3: blue pants, belt, work shirt,
        topsiders to work boots
I-4: green pants, belt, sport shirt, topsiders
I-5: blue pants, belt, work shirt, work boots
I-6: Same as above plus sports jacket
I-7: (quick change) brown slacks, shirt, tie,
        sports jacket, loafers
II-1: Same as above
II-3 through II-4: brown work pants, shirt,
        work boots
II-5: (quick change) blue dress shirt, tie,
        2 piece suit, loafers

Yens Undershirt, black socks, wedding ring
I-1 through I-5: pants, suspenders, shirt,
        slippers
I-6: add robe
I-7: add sweater
II-1 through II-3: pajamas and robe, slippers

HANDBOOK

for

THEATRICAL APPRENTICES
By Dorothy Lee Tompkins

Here is a common sense book on theatre, fittingly sub-titled, "A Practical Guide in All Phases of Theatre." Miss Tompkins has wisely left art to the artists and written a book which deals only with the practical side of the theatre. All the jobs of the theatre are categorized, from the star to the person who sells soft drinks at intermission. Each job is defined, and its basic responsibilities given in detail. An invaluable manual for every theatre group in explaining to novices the duties of apprenticeship, and in reassessing its own organizational structure and functions.

"If you are an apprentice or are just aspiring in any capacity, then you'll want to read and own Dorothy Lee Tompkins' A HANDBOOK FOR THEATRICAL APPRENTICES. It should be required reading for any drama student anywhere and is a natural for the amateur in any phase of the theatre."—George Freedley, Morning Telegraph.

"It would be helpful if the HANDBOOK FOR THE-ATRICAL APPRENTICES were in school or theatrical library to be used during each production as a guide to all participants."—Florence E. Hill, Dramatics Magazine.

HOME-BUILT

Lighting Equipment

for The Small Stage

By THEODORE FUCHS

This volume presents a series of fourteen simplified designs for building various types of stage lighting and control equipment, with but one purpose in mind—to enable the amateur producer to acquire a complete set of stage lighting equipment at the lowest possible cost. The volume is 8½" x 11" in size, with heavy paper and spiral binding—features which make the volume well suited to practical workshop use.

Community Theatre

A MANUAL FOR SUCCESS

By JOHN WRAY YOUNG

The ideal text for anyone interested in participating in Community Theatre as a vocation or avocation. "Organizing a Community Theatre," "A Flight Plan for the Early Years," "Programming for People—Not Computers," and other chapters are blueprints for solid growth. "Technical, Business and Legal Procedures" cuts a safe and solvent path through some tricky undergrowth. Essential to the library of all community theatres, and to the schools who will supply them with talent in the years to come.